OMENS IN THE YEAR OF THE OX

For Jess-
with high expectations for
your own first collection,
which will come.

- PIVOT - TORONTO -
. 2a2 .

OMENS IN THE YEAR OF THE OX

poems

STEVEN PRICE

Brick Books

Library and Archives Canada Cataloguing in Publication

Price, Steven, 1976-
    Omens in the year of the ox / Steven Price.

Poems.
ISBN 978-1-926829-76-0

    I. Title.

PS8631.R524O64 2012   C811'.6   C2011-908120-2

We acknowledge the Canada Council for the Arts, the Government of Canada through the Canada Book Fund, and the Ontario Arts Council for their support of our publishing program.

Cover design by Michel Vrana.

The author photo was taken by Esi Edugyan.

The book is set in Bembo.

Design and layout by Alan Siu.

Printed and bound by Sunville Printco Inc.

Brick Books
431 Boler Road, Box 20081
London, Ontario N6K 4G6

www.brickbooks.ca

For Jacqueline, old friend

Contents

II

III

We pass these things on,
probably, because we are what we can imagine.
Robert Hass

The Crossing

I

So. At the end of the middle of your life
you wake, rain-shivering, to a white railing
in a shriven dusk. A strangeness churning
under the hull, the great blades boiling through
ferruginous waters. So the ferries sail still
in this late age, vast holds half-full of souls.
And so you rise, each day, more than you were.
Exhausted, maybe, into silence. When Bridges
wrote, *How is the world's bright shift held*
in such a cluttered line? Hopkins, in a rage,
had no answer. Or none beyond his poetry.
Rain in silver ropes overrunning his faith,
his metre marking long great gulps of night air.
So the waters gulp at the mournful hull,
so the rusted bolts bleed. You unfold both
fists in the charred coastal dusk, watching
a white chill krill across their skin. Bright shift,
cluttered line. If the ill of the world issues
up out of the world, then there is no course
but to praise it. As Hopkins praised it. In the straits
a slack foam froths blackly in the scum, and you
who are water stare at that water, blurred
by old hurts praise holds no part in, here
at the edge of a dark crossing that is always
evening. As if called to account for a life
lived in the provinces. But there is no
calling to account. You sway at a railing
staring west, towards desolation, that is, forgetting.

II

In Gaudí's Palau Güell, with her. How the walls
wept into form, as you wandered hall to hall
in that black building, astonished such a shape
could hold. The built thing made bright shift of.
Gaudí had given Güell an allegory of the cross,
both sculpture and story. It was a spatial truth
he'd sought: an ascension up, up
seven stories towards the spires of heaven.
That cellar with its termitic columns,
that cellar where partisans were tortured,
that cellar of sand, dust, stone: that was Hell.
You rested under the white shards of pottery
on Gaudí's rooftop, watching a white cat pour
past her ankles like blood-threaded milk
while a red sun drenched the staggered chimneys.
How she looked at you, suddenly perplexed.
And when you asked, *What is it?* she laughed,
having just forgotten what it was. *Nothing,*
she said, meaning everything she already had.
There is your desire, and her desire, and each
touches many things. You carried Hopkins
all through Spain, wanting to get closer
to something. His stark Jesuit suffering, perhaps.
Tracing your burned fingers along the cool
ancient stones in the narrow streets
of the Gothic Quarter, his music
in your head. We believe we are living
one life and learn too late we have been
living another, she said. If all our pasts
are possible pasts then we are no kind of gone.

On Gaudí's tiled roof she pointed past a line
of smoky blue spires in the Barcelona haze,
and you felt your future darken before you.
Does it matter now if none of that is true?
You know that you cannot, maybe, bring her
into that city, where she was not. Still, there
she waits, as you waited, under the locked
iron grillwork of the Palau Güell, sick
with absence, which was the real crossing,
and was in everything, and is, and has no end.

III

The smoky waters are the still sour yellow
of poisoned milk. A brooding sky recedes.
At the stern a ragged passenger perches,
collar rolled cold against a windblown dawn,
almost her. You shade your eyes, look away.
Frenzied light, sea like crumpled foil—
the world burns redly up out of the strait,
silent, and vague, and sinister, like a dream
interrupted. You had been reading about love
and evil, how the one would transcend
death and the other deny it. Death
being both bright shift and the upwelling.
So your shadow ducks the deck's edge
to shatter in the spray, and so you go
back, going back. To the monster that stalked her
through a clattering train carriage in Catalonia,
who shuffled like an old man, who shouldered
no luggage, blue eyes half-kind as he stared

her into meat, trembling with age and what
already had been done and what he would
do again. Evil is its own element,
and real, it pours from itself like a sea, all flux,
whole and divisionless and without center.
When next you see her she will not, it's true,
be who she was. You watch night bell murkily,
fathoms down, sinking deeper; at the far rail
a faint sun flares, its vicious hooks flowing
round you and in you, clutching for purchase.
In the swells the grizzled gulls glide and cry.
She will never, will never, will never die.

IV

What is steadfast? Nothing is steadfast. You
sailed for the desired world, remembering.
How Gaudí's friend and patron, Güell, died
of a burst heart in 1918, and the works fell still.
Fierce, shabby Gaudí. Shuffling into decay.
That was the year Bridges dredged up his dead
friend Hopkins' forced and gnarled verses,
in a brief embarrassed print run. Few copies
survive; the poems go on. What is steadfast?
Sunlight shivers on the face
of the imperceptible now, as if in answer.

V

In the end all is a river that flows from fog
to fog, that darkens the selves within us.
In the end, for the tides, this world is the world
it was. So the waters recede and recede,
so you trudge out after them, hopeless.
Trusting a far shore exists. *Absolute*
love, wrote Bridges from the long drift
of his fame, *is measured hour by hour.*
Where I say hours I mean years, mean life,
wrote Hopkins. All of us arrive, somehow,
in the here. The black firs loom and pass
in the cold light of the crossing. Far out,
gulls drift and disarticulate in the grey,
their song an ugly, rasping appetite.
As it is in all of us. The final waters,
fanged and liquid, open under our feet.
Who wrote that? A Spanish poet, most likely.
You remember walking the fragrant lanes
of Mojácar at dusk, the lemon trees belling
low over the orchard walls. As you crossed
a corner into a gulch a huge darkness
detached itself from the ditch and glided
growling out, all sinew and razored shadow
blocking the middle of the end of that road.
Its black hackles bristling. And you understood:
you could go no further.

Field Guide to the Sanctuary

I

A grey lagoon searing dark
with chill winds. Rockstrewn
strands lashed and scoured.

What eddies here wants
no mercy. Is salt and savage.
Snub-blunt and sculling

the grey gulls punch
their weight in the spray, lift,
hang over humped middens

shingled to chalk-shell,
shaled and cold. Watch
their world wheel under.

II

I have seen this, seen
this. The dart and snaking
barb of swans at feed.

A slow child swarmed
by slithers of char-geese, dragged
howling into black water.

The folded plunging incision
of hawks in the wash;
feathers scalpelling the air,

sharpening. Look dead
in any eye: terror
clockworks there.

III

A mallard's worm-
swaying skull swivots, stabs,
plicks at greased gun-

feathers underwing. A wind rises:
the steel waters sheen and chop.
One gull swells up, is blown

like a plastic bag out over the drop;
most wait out the worst
huddled grim. The world

here is harsh, guttural, or still.
Threnody plays no part.
On an outcrop, now, kneel,

observe the birds' ferocious art.

Odysseus and the Sirens

Here
    their
fear
    churned
him hard;
that scarred
smoke-glarred
    strand burned

like black shell;
his men held
their ears well-
    stogged with wax
and cut, dipped, dragged
through froth oarblades,
old shafts gone grey—
    their knuckled backs

wracked by hard rowing—
as, lashed fast, flowing
with rope and roping
    his muscles in knots
of their own cording, he,
Odysseus, hung; leaned
low, gasping at that beam,
    bloodied ears shunted shut—

when came the breached dream out of the sea.

    Scorched wharves. Slit fish noonspackled with heat:
Now was this land that he knew; now surging on past could he make out
    white hills, sunhammered, walls hazed in the blur

and his eyes afire hawked fast, hunted *her*—

not this, nothingness, this
no-song of wind and hiss
and spray, gulls in tall gusts
    shoaling over shore rocks—
in that rain-flared chop
their oars, all surge and scup
of salt-stripped cedar, stopped;
    he stared back in shock:

a battered beach,
kelp-strangled, seethed
with mysteries
    and wind-amped cries
damp with want;
he shook then;
he, ropes rent,
    shut his eyes—

that land
of stunned
black sand
    was love:
shore
    our
horrors
    sing of.

Chorus

In they'd drift, almost motes, like echoes

of the eye, like articles of dust

stirred in the drapes' dreary pall.

"See with the eye," they admonished,

"and seeming will be less and less."

"He has no ear for longing,"

sighed one, or was it: "He hears no air

of longing"? I screeled clear the drapes

on tarnished rods, seeing neither shape

nor shroud. "See," said another,

"he sees nothing not his own."

"We are his own." "Or were his own."

Knuckling shut my eyes to caulk shut

my skull. "He thinks he can ignore us,"

one hissed; "this singing he signed on for

never had sense in it." "Stubborn."

For God's sake, I muttered, *I can hear you,*

I'm here, I'm right here—

At which each silvered into blessed silence.

I listened to the sweet nothing

adrift in the drapes. But then:

"Did he just say he's right?" "Right here."

"Who is he?" "What is right?"

"Where is here?"

Jarred Pears under Dust

A man's bruised hand glows

like glass. Unthreads the lid,
pries back the brass cap
in a wet suck of icy air.
Jarred pears drift in flecks

of what serene fire, drift
burning with what sweetness.
In any jar an inner autumn
rises: calved pears float

pure, float white; and a boy's
bruised hand pours out
light. We walk a heavy
orchard all our days

to watch such white fruit fade.

Icarus in the Tower

As if winched in harness
he works late, his withered desk's
worn olive-wood blurred—
works, all wax and bristling
quill in the murky wine-dark shine.

O my strange, sad father.
How he does not see me.
Tangled in the bars of our cell
the lyred tendons
of dried seabirds

stretch, or split, or dangle
over scrolls we sketched for lift.
I lie like a coal in the dark straw
seething with light.
I stare and stare.

He shuffles forth
in his frail creaking contraption
of leather-twined harness,
rib-crossed strap. In candlefire,
clips the brass buckles fast,

the wings soft in the smoky burn.
Then turns; mutters; widens
the twiggy light-as-bone
wingspan of his wattled arms.
I watch his slack underskin shine.

It is not the flesh that first must fly.
When he stoops blacking the light,
bat-winged and magnificent,
how I fear for him, fear
he lacks the recklessness

this act will ask of us. All my life
I have lived in shadow knowing light
does not keep. Knowing
what falls to the son. All night
now each night I watch

the exquisite wax smoulder and weep.

The Wrecking

It falls. All week
    the high whine, ping
of steel bolts screed
    down to shearings,

shafts. That hotel
    gutted to its eaves
leans, fenced-off out
    a mud-straked street

where red dust blown
    through rust-thick air
blooms, like fear;
    it leans, a slow

huge whooshed insuck
    of gust and crash—
then falls. All brick,
    mortar, glass, ash.

Where the wet gashed
    works groan, gape wide,
men wade the slash:
    flexed girders grind

hard, arc-rolled steel
    rods clang; and dust
being all, all
    is dragged to dust.

Under that dark
    and blood-slaked sun
dark smoke rises.
    This world too will end.

Chorus

Two ghosted, I guess, in, goldening maybe

where the bells of gleaming pans wavered

in racks above the stove. I let them talk.

"He fears the surest work's the least assured;

looks to the burning of the useless, at least

the burning off of it." "That's the ash of it."

The kitchen cantled with, what, an ambered shine,

as if a candle burned in sunlight. Was that them?

"He trusts us." "No; he trusts to a singing

which seduces; he sings his meaning."

"But picks apart the clockwork to while away

the time. While none of it means a thing."

And if, say, one trusted nothing, least of all

the singing? As the table's grain coalesced

in a honeyed light, so little seemed

to matter. "How assured he sounds," sighed one.

"Sure as faith," agreed some aggrieved

second. I knew it wasn't possible to live

in faith without living too in doubt. "Assured

again," they whispered, "doubly so, and so

reassured." At which I reached for a knife

and calmly began to carve the bread.

Danube Relic

As if its brown charred tip once tapped
hard this hauled-stone

cathedral's crypt, once wanted out.
Seems a saint's relic

scraped in soiled wrappers outweeps
even guarded glass:

see its slow molten dreep dap low.
So like wax creeping.

Was a girl's once. And once curled
tangles of lace

from her living face what's now all char
and tallow-grease,

black drip and blur burned centuries
past. Latched under glass

her shrivelled finger, survived of fire,
graces a gilt cord,

hangs hacked, weathered, grey-tethered and tied
like a twist of grass

left to dry. Papered like a wasps' nest,
tarred nail tapered,

it's said held hard her finger feels it yet—
half hook-and-wire,

all sawed-off strange, the hand of a girl burned
burns like fire.

Auto-da-Fé

Grace is like fire, says Augustine of Hippo, extending the metaphor: burning a man must be done with skill if he is to last. Most die with merely their calves on fire. I remember a dark swale of grass, a girl lifting her shirt. Folding back her cuffs to show her scars. Cigarette burns in small white lesions on her wrists. When burning a man, one must tether faggots and twists of straw up the stake to the head. In this way he will burn in stages and not be overwhelmed. She ran her fingers through her hair and her hair in the dusk was singed by the fire of that setting sun. As a toddler Augustine had played in the courtyard while his mother bathed, the bones glowing in her ankles. Augustine says in the sunlight the hands of our mothers burn like sunlight, like they aren't there at all. It is never what we think. She rubbed her scars and said, *Fire eats and eats in order not to die.* I said, *We are so alike you and I.*

Bull Kelp

The weed is dark inside and wetbrained.

All night drifts down cold waters,
lolls like a child's skull in the swells

then washes up here: unboned eelthing,
stiff searoot, tough resined tentacle

risen from what brackish dream.
Drained to sand-pocked rubber, dried

ochre, dried grey, its slack blades
splay from a shrivelled stalk

like the bent stump of some blunt propeller,
mangled in bladderwrack and reeking.

Embrangled, yes, rucked, yes, battered
by that bright element we too wake to,

come dawn dead kelp sprawls
cold with the nightcold and so stiff

its uncoiled mess, massed, won't shift
at a kick. Now sandfleas blink like blown sparks out;

now hauled hard by the brunted head
its stipe, whip-sharp, hists a wet sigh

and the sun bells redly through its blades.
What a thing it is. Evidence perhaps.

Cast up thickening among us
to bleach here in a burning air, stretched

long, long, gleeched and ungulous
until it, this, stewed placenta, this puddled thing

poked with a stick or walked unwondering past
splits its slippery gutline, peels apart in rot—

and a knot of larvae boils in that dark and does not clot.

Arbutus

If grief were given shape, if grief
were given shape would it grow like this

in a horror of limbs, and headless—

Abruptly up to gripped rock it
gives, groan on ingrained

groan, it

writhes, waterworn and weathering
the weather of its own wood

while the shelf of the world shivers.

No bark
is born so old. No bark is born

with blunt teeth bared and tearing red strips of itself

in such thin streaping curls of skin, no bark
but this, crackling under the smooth gnarl

of its own flensing. Windlorn, windflinted,

still like slow molasses wound on a stick
it pours the thick thrust of itself

hugely upward, anguished, arboreal,

it seeks its brutal purchase, it sinks its rootmuscles in
and will not be moved, it will be

unmoved

as if grief as if grief as if
grief, engorged, grappled its roots below. No it has no

choice. It outstrips itself as it grows.

A Gloss on *Arbutus*

I stood under it, stunned.
Ropes of red hair in its rails.
Its leaves, sundialed, shone.
My skull rigged open like a sail.

I swung under it, stunned.
The world in its shook foil shone.
I was an eye and was not.
What I wanted was undone.

The unbeautiful was fraught.
I watched a punched branch spin.
My wrists, sundialed, shone.
When I gasped a gust rushed in.

Then all was gloom, appalled bark, and my arms were swaying with wind.

Raccoon in Ditch

I

Where seed-foaming weeds drag darkly, dusk rises;
    rises in a last crunch of sunlight off fenders flaring west—

you watch each tiny plicked claw stutter shut.
    Asplayed, astunned, so unskinned it seems

but gleetslicked gut: innards peeled back like a glove
    lately worn, warm yet. Blood-dazed, black ants swarm

like a hive of darkness. What you feel is love:
    how all things that live have inner halls light knows nothing of.

How you are also of that dark.

II

    Dragged from what black dream running, hurtled
to what weed-ditch. Grey fur bloodrubbed at its ribs
    and, seamsplit, that slow blue bubble of gut.

    A dead raccoon is dull and like any other
dead goes stiff in its own thingness. Sticks can't shift it.
    Wasps lift past it low in the pollen-stung air.

    Less than that it seems. Unzippered, a purse of fur
poured from itself. Gorged fat on dayfire and grown
    beyond all size. Scraped up, a bucket's worth.

But lumbering thick-shanked, fur-thighed, once
its banded tail dragged fatly like a bull's phallus;
    at dusk would slouch through a clatter of cans

    what sprawls now spoiling in groil and ooze, snout
fanged yet, lips flensed back, flecked fur frothing with ants—
    what once could drown a hound thrice its weight.

    What are they. Night-diggers, weasel-gods, furred moons:
seen afar, they peer at us with the green eyes of children;
    come dusk their delicate hands could be human.

                            III

    How you are also of that dark.

How all things that live have inner halls light knows nothing of,
    like hives of darkness. What you feel is love

lately worn, warm with blood. Black ants swarm;
    all gleetslicked gut, innards peeled back like a glove,

asplayed, astunned, and so unskinned it seems
    you are not you. Tiny plicked claws stutter shut

in a crunch and flare of sunlight; fenders fade west;
    and there, where seed-foaming weeds drag low, something

rises. There will be no other end to the world.

Chorus

I drove through furred fields veiled in rain

when road struck sea struck sky. Parked

brooding above the windscried chop

of a weedchoked beach, watched one

shudder through a shut vent in the dash.

"It's dark in here," it whispered, "dark

as pitch." "Darker," another hissed,

forming in the back. "Dark as meaning."

"Dark as love." Others were drifting in.

"The kelp down there's dark inside

and wetbrained," said one. I sat

outshivering the chill, jacket slack

and thin. *You have nothing to say,* I said,

your words are without meaning.

A silence; then muttering soft as felt.

"Who's he speaking to?" "He's alone."

You believe in nothing, I added, as the wet

light warpled where I clutched the wheel.

Then the air stilled; they addressed me

directly. "It's as you fear. Our voices are just

vowels jarred to clattering, errors

mucked with meaning. You know this

and knew this. The emptiness you fear

is speaking in you; what you hear

is the nothing that nothing announces."

And then, to drive their point clear:

"You are not haunted. Nothing is in you."

Reparations

Juliet onstage in Florence sheathing a blade in her breast.
How she wept, in Italian, in black weather. That was the
third night. All day we had crossed museum halls, our
steps echoing from that famous statue's broken embrace
to a faded canvas baring Helen's dagger of white thigh.
It seems our greatest arguments for love are all arguments
against it. The sun was going down and the pigeons were
inking the cobblestones of the square. There was a child
wearing an accordion. He sang, We do not remember a time
before we were loved. Hearts, too, are tuned to a minor key
and like other instruments hang mostly silent, collecting dust. I
was born on a Thursday. On a Thursday six men carved a hole
in my grandfather's chest, removed and jarred and preserved
his bad heart like bruised fruit. Remember always the heart is a
made thing, the child sang. In the manner of music or fire, the
crowds sang back. We are shaped by human hands and what
loves us consumes us.

Bach's Soprano

Feeds and feeds.

Eats air, ear, all: her white throat
thoraxing where waxed lamps flare;

where six thousand silver ears dial
in darkness dreamily towards her.
Soft faces stunned by such light.

No shame in sitting stunned
among the stunned, slumped in gloom.
That hall's high ribbed shell gleams;

my difficult friend, I lean
along a low felt armrest and accept,
since it is real, my own failing

ambition on this earth. All is
emptied. She sings a vast engulfing intake
of air, wrenched and vocable,

when again the vortex takes her,
drains her. Feeds, feeds on a fading world.
That a thing so fragile persists,

that a thing so fragile is heard. You
watch the white shine of an ear in the dark
fade. We live and are diminished.

Orpheus Ascending

Blood-deep in black rock: a keyhole
    blazing like the silver ear
of a god. A door. He staggered cold
    and shaking through the cellar
of an old villa: racks of grimy bottles
straked in soot, char, ash; that grotto's
           dank air
           stirred, flared
its dust like golden krill in his weird stare

where the black reek of brackish meat
    hazed him yet. His lungs burned
with the dark sweetness of it, her,
    the stink of wet soil and her
rot in his skin, harp, clothes. Dragged
back from daylight, her ragged
           black hair
           bruised there,
her grey sluckish flesh shuddering to air

ten steps shy of the world— Hell
    in its green darkness was not hell;
here the cold villa of the real hell
    flensed him, he shivered: hell
was sighting her soft shrivelled head
slick with a fungal rot, her bled
           lips moist,
           limbs poised,
swaying like the blind in the lantern of his voice

even as he turned. All of it, all
        was a kind of rot, it ate the skin—
He straggled upstairs, through halls,
        courtyards, into the weak sun
singing yet. Fearing what he'd wanted.
But, too: how lovely, how haunted
                his voice
                    was, is—
when he felt her footsteps falter under his.

Hard yellow wasps in the weeds at his hips.
        Dried grapes on stakes. Then the earth
shuddered under, shirred, his heart slipped
        and his lips were smeared with dirt,
the thick black mulch churning there: it seemed
some evil thing in that earth was singing,
                singing,
                    singing,
something evil in that earth was singing.

II

The Tunnel

Now that we have cleared the last bricks, it is time. All month we laboured in a smoky lamplight, groping wearily while our brothers slept above us in their cells. The rafters creaking overhead as they stirred. And each dawn, called to matins, how we prayed silently for fortitude, for grace: *Lord guide us now in this our late trace.* See the cellar boards, peeled back with care, propped across the dusty casks: even their charred nails point us earthwards. Is it the devil's work we do? This hole holds a thick and oily shadow even lampshine cannot cut. Kneeling before it, we sometimes smell leaf-mould, sometimes honey, sometimes only a cold wind that plucks at our sleeves.

Yesterday in chapel the chalice split in two.

Soon now we go through.

Midwife's Curses

May your sons be born
    grey, blood-slathered in thick sludge;
may they never cry.

————————

May you love only deeply
    and never die.

————————

May blood glut your breasts—
      may all you eat be dust in your mouth,
    ash in the mouths of your kin.

————————

May your milk be a ribbon of darkness,
    your lullabies a black wind.

————————

May you wake weeping to your life
    each morning:
  may what is hidden keep ever hidden.

————————

May everything be permitted you.
May nothing be forbidden.

————————

May your sons devour their daughters,
    your daughters dash their sons to the floor;
may each foetus feed in you like cancer.

————————

May your prayers be answered.

The Tyrant's Physician

Since you ask: like a viscous blue jellyfish, its tendrils adrift. That is how his wife's eye swims in that vase. Come; fetch me the colder basin. This heat could boil apart the bones of a lamb. His headaches? Oh, he is luminous with pain. They will not be cured by tea leaves or figs. He is dying, wattling into a husk. He can no longer bear the red sun in the morning corridors, and he does not dream at all. Do you imagine it is guilt? He said to me: *I have learned that the suffering of others does not exist.* He said: *At night in the faint frescoes I begin to see.* Oh, such things he sees! I cannot begin to tell you. Yesterday he stood at the window and told me: *You would like to be useful, yes? In the courtyard, that blonde child polishing the stones. Bring her to me.*

Medea

She cradled her ale like an infant's head,
dragged it close. Glass all aglar and rasping

in her palms – thumbfogged, pubthick –
rolling slow on its heel where she gripped it

grinding wet half-moons dark in the bar's grain.
"Did you think something would go through me?"

she asked, thick-lidded eyes hooded in that haze;
"and what then? a bolt? an arrow?" She clicked

the brown heft of her glass hard down.
Our waitress loomed, threading her tray

asway in the smoke and roar; then swift
as a god-from-the-machine deposited another.

"So let it come," she said, "by my hand
or his. O he'll suffer for what he's done.

I swear it on the throats of our children."
Drilling her hard knuckle through the cork;

that scarred oak table etched with what
old love initialed there, long since stubbed

out, scrubbed, scoured, stogied-out
until no longer any's name. "My name, this,

Medea, will never mean sweetness or milk.
I gave birth and was gutted. A mother knows

what that means." I said nothing. A slap
of doors behind the bar, rattle of dishes clattering

off the drainpan beyond. She was crying now.
"Love should leave the world the way it came."

She did not need to say what way that was.

———————

Innocence is incorruptible. They drift.
Let it live everlasting. And dream.
Dead is not dead, what does not perish:
a candle clutched in her fists like a blade
as she watches their little chests fall.
This is not the world she made. O her
delicate sons, more than mere reflection,
each lies blurred like a curl of smoke
in sheets where she'd made them in love.
Love, she spits, crushing out the flame.
They will be sheltered even from love.

―――――――

We braked. Geared south in a slur of dust,
gattled stones spattering the pitted wells
where tread-rubber rode hot in the grooved hull.
And pulled slow off. A station gone to rust:

twin scabby pumps squatting desolate, bleary
in the day's heat-hover. She'd thought return
might mean a turn to rights, lessons learned.
But banked by black cliffs, bleached eyries eerie

with no wing or cry, that shut gas bar seemed
no end to what we'd sought, or once had thought to be.

★

Still a stunned bell banged out as we pulled in.
We had gone as far as this. For what. No word.
And slumped now rustburnt as a man emerged
griming his hands in a rag. That look we gave him

strange as he cocked the gauge, lugged the gun,
punched the trigger to full. Bent at our hood,
his rag just smearing the grease and roadslime round
when with a sudden ache in that splintering sun

we saw it. A well of darkness, whorling up in him:
how what overspills our lives is not if but when.

★

His weird visage shivered watery, blurred
behind a slap of ropy cloth: blearing the glass
to bad effect, spiralling a foul grey wash
of soap deeper in. The day darkened under.

Then came the savaging, the voice of the god.
"Did she think something would go through her?"
it groaned at me. "She is no vessel. Nothing's in her
that was not ever in her. She will know blood,

her own blood, shed. All births bring the same:
gore, fear, screams; small limbs wrenched in pain—

★

she will bear it." Then he was back, shining a mirror,
scrubbing out glass that the road ahead come clear.

———————

Three dreams she dreamed back to back.
First: twin boulders of bread, broken apart,
which she ripped in warm fistfuls of crust.
Her wrists agleam in a heartblinding shine.
Love, spare us the bitter and hesitant life:
that dream sheathed its secret in her
ribs like a knife. In the second dream
two crackling sails, torn in a wind, flailed
where a white moon waned into gloom.
Shadow unmakes what the shining once made:
everything is vanishing, though it take
an age to disappear. The third dream
was no dream and from it she would not wake.

—————————

Then did Medea lead down to the shed.

Haltingly, legs alurch, leaden in thick woolen
skirts. As if looped in a sharp steel line

that led inward. A bulb's red filament
flared, glowed to slow life: light, asway

in the rippled tin walls, sliding off tools
tacked up toothed and cold like instruments

of cruelty. I stood at the edge in darkness.
She slung a snubbed hammer by its claw, stared

dully back at the shack where both boys slept.
That greasy smell of her hair, grimed, sour

like bad milk; in her eyes, a cadaverous heart.
"Medea," I said. "You can still stand aside.

Nothing's written that can't be changed."
Turning, her scalp bashed the bulb: shadows

spun, swirled, skitted back. "You only want it so,"
she scowled. "My mistakes were cast

at every turning. I chose always him."
And then in half-anger at herself, or me:

"You'll get this wrong; you'll tell it wrong."
Back in the dark shack a phone was ringing

but pitched strange, too shrill, shrieking
like a saw shivering into bone. "It's the second

night," I told her. "He might still return."
Lifting a hatchet, hefting its haft, setting it

back. She did set it back. The phone shrieked
and shrieked. She stumbled out, I assumed,

to answer it, as I stood in that sinister shed;
the shrieking seemed to go on a long time;

then it stopped and the air went dead.

Ghosts

According to reports, during the closing days of the Second World War, residents of the Austrian village of Kosse were rounded up, marched into a nearby copse of birches, and shot through the base of the skull. The soldiers responsible, billeted in the houses of the murdered, almost immediately began to complain of certain unusual events. Silverware, furniture, dishes would move in the night; shoelaces and socks would vanish; small pieces of food would be found sorted along the mantels of fireplaces, in front of heating vents, under bookshelves. Footsteps, slamming doors, soft weeping, thumps in the walls: such disturbances continued until 1964, when one of the houses was gutted for renovations. Workmen, tearing open a brick wall in the attic, discovered a small grey man living in the wall. In hiding since 1940, he had over the years excavated a complex passage of tunnels through the walls and floors. When they carried him out he lay on the stretcher shrivelled and hairless and frightened. It seems he had not realized the war had ended. Since that time, thirty-seven other survivors have been discovered. Unhappily, however, the hauntings continue.

Gardener's Curses

May black waters stunt your children,
your taps run brackish and impure.

—————————

May your stalks rot to sticks;
may the roots endure.

—————————

May your labours be laid
in clay, sand, rock, bog;

may all your fruit be wormfall,
  your orchards sown with salt.

—————————

May you sleep long and late;
may you wake with fingers
  smooth as cream.

—————————

And may the weather that shines
    be outshone ever
  by the weather you dream.

—————————

May you be blessed with many neighbours;
may their harvests run high.

—————————

And may a white sun burn burn burn
  in an ever cloudless sky.

Three Blues

I. SWEET MISS MOLLY GRINN

Sure sir he left me an he left me nothin—
just a tub of jelly,
a big ol belly,
an I aint seen my man now two nights runnin.
       Aw that old razor aint nothin to see.

Steeled hisself up, set his ol self down—
like a old white bandage
when the bad's at you;
I said I aint seen my man two nights runnin.
       Aw that old razor aint nothin to see.

Said last I seen's black back of his head; said
aint leave nothin, said
no dough no bread;
just a ol tarnish ring said he give me if he dead.
       No that old razor aint nothin to see.

Well good's to the girl got to know what's what—
but if he aint own up,
he aint own up,
an man better make sure he know how it cut.
       Aw that old razor aint nothin to see.

II. VAGRANCY BLUES

Got to lurk,
shine an shirk,
aint nothin so sweet as steady work.
      Got to thank the man.

Got sun, sand,
coalblack tan,
an ever man workin just as hard as he can.
      Got to thank the man.

Got bed, board,
ten to a ward,
shiny new collar for each of us, lord—
      Got to thank the man.

Got time, time,
askin no dime,
punchin that dirt on God's county line.
      Got to thank the man.

Ever day,
night an day,
watchin the good man give us our pay—
      O right proper one a these days
      we goin to thank that man,
      I say we goin to thank that man.

III. DARK TRAIN SONG

This train it leavin Boston, sixty-seven soul alive.
This train it leavin Boston, sixty-seven soul alive.
But when it get to Oakham, just sixty-six soul arrive.

See this train it dark in tunnels, grey man got a wife.
This train it dark in tunnels, grey man got a wife.
But her train aint goin to Oakham; grey man bring a knife.

Goin cut her in her belly, goin cut her in her throat.
Goin cut her in her belly, goin slit her sweet black throat.
Till those iron rusted rails run all bloody underfoot.

O aint no evil in the valley, aint no evil in the town.
No aint no evil in the valley, aint no evil in the town.
But ride them old blue rails boy it ever can be found.

The Inferno

Speculation suggests it might be, must be, hell. A vast cavern unearthed deep under Baffin Island. Experts are puzzled by both its location and its depth. Last week two exploratory crews were dispatched. We are told the first drillers passed trembling into a huge and silent blackness, while a wind reeking of sulphur crackled in the tunnels around the second, wailing like the cries of the dead. It seems the caverns funnel ever deeper, descending through chasms and sheer drops. The first crew photographed windcarved mineral spires, twisted like shrivelled oaks. When they shone their lamps on the walls, the slick burned luminous and blue. Great silver cathedrals of limestone arched far into the depths. At their innermost point, the second crew discovered a stone well; its depth has not yet been determined. Under a bench near its edge they found a pair of rotted wood sandals, and a small leather psalter printed in Genoa.

All who have returned agree the beauty of those caverns rivals Rome

Curses of the Blind

May you see the world as it is
    in its darkness;
may night be your day.

————————

May you never look away.

————————

May you learn the hour of your death
              early;
may its wind on your face be foul.

————————

May you fall, and fall, and fall, and fall.

————————

May all your seeing be foreseeing;
and may you mistake
    becoming for being.

————————

May the road to your gate
be thicketed
    and steep.

————————

And O may you never sleep.

————————

May your halls shirr with whispers,
        the creaking of frightened feet—
may your wife's weeping outlast
even sky, even grass.

——————————

May all the ills you wished on others
come to pass.

Omens at the Edge

That was ebb tide in the breaches,
gulls shrieking
in the spin. We waded in:

chilled mud windgilled, sifting
under us with wash,
the black barnacled rocks slick

as the slate waters fell back
and the world receded to sand.
Call it kind's clarity

of purpose. Call it the going
out. Not to wade too far
past treefall, landfall, light,

lest our darker selves
rise roiling in the white
breakers combing inward,

and know us as we were: here
where no one's ever one
person, and a curtain

rent in the wide shimmer
and the shorn light
of the long ago already was

creaking to its rusty close.

We entered that distance;
we entered our diminishing.

III

The Excursion

Once onshore we shuddered to see it: like panic pouring over the dead
    shale, the shellfused
rockpools, it oozed
    its hooded head
under a barnacled block
    in a smooth crush
of coils, was flushed
    black-muscled back
through the cold flail
    of its beak, a soft vent
murking a current;
    then gulped a bell
of ink against the glassed
    surface and fell
still. Each slow gasp welled
    up strange to us
where we crouched. Smaller than
    we'd thought it, it
slewed, limbs knotted
    like knuckled hands
wrung white, a sight
    we saw and shrank from—
who had not come
    for this. The sea light
wimpled like banged steel
    in the beyond.
We rose. Reeled stunned
    in a reeking squall
of sandflies, saltburnt decay;
    then, like appalled
reflections of half-recalled

lives, turned away.
"What was it?" asked
    one; "a fish?" "Not
a fish," we replied; "not
    that." And thought: *ghost*.
That soft horror pulsed
    on in its rockpool
like an ember
    of darkness; we left it
there. And, slow, trudged
    down the rock-ledge
our low craft lifted
    in the shadow of, lifted
and fell from. The light
    was failing. Our guide
hunched astern, hooded,
    knuckling white oars.
He lifted his face.
    It seemed we did
not know this place;
    and if we woke
we would remember
    none of this.

Dream of the Fisherman's Wife

Which once more unwaked from drags down all
she is: grey-shawled, cold, in a dark parlour
she waits, her small white hands salt-stung still.
The night oysters in tight around her. Colder
black winds shoal hard her latched gate;
its nothing all week wakes her. She shuts
her eyes. Tells herself he's moored-up late
or gutting yet the catch, the slurred fish slit
and flaring in the drainpans' phosphor tin,
plicked scales quick on slickers greased with gore—
men are late for any reason. Now wind
bangs up the back porch like a boy soaked bare.
She does not think of last week. Its downpour.
The drenched men gaffing that body to shore.

Omens in the Year of the Ox

The lake slits its belly; a pale blade slips in.
All oared elbow,

black back-kick and purl, all sputtered gasp of froth-
sprayed shine blown out,

she, slack, cuts through pitch, wrists dragging a deeper cold.
Old stars swim out over.

Treading the dead waters, she goes out. Grey hair adrift,
flected and lucent

there where each slow reach, gasp, roll, reach of her
churns and churns what

sleeps in her wake. When she wades out the shallows
drain off her fingers

in slow molten ingots; her ankles bloom in the tarred silt
and she's shivering—

a thing flowing fathoms under had finned up past her
there in the black,

a thing vast, stirred, deep, ancient and cold, utterly
unconcerned with her

had slurred along her flesh in a long silvering flash,
a living current,

then plunged back down to the dark and was lost.

The Persian General

Herodotus tells us that when the tyrant Arximedes learned that Polygoras, whose verses were admired even among the Persians, stood among his captives, he summoned him to dine. In the firelight he unbound the Greek's hands and offered wine, fresh bread, oysters in mountain ice. He laid a jewelled finger on the poet's wrist. "I would like you to sing of my victories," he said, "I would like you to march with me." The Greek refused. Arximedes cajoled, pleaded, threatened, charmed. But when he realized his captive could not be persuaded, the tyrant released him and sent him stumbling off towards the Greek lines. He would not extinguish such a light from the world, Herodotus writes admiringly, even though it burn against him. The following morning Arximedes cut out the tongues and noses from the remaining prisoners, then flayed each man alive. Three hundred twenty-six captive Greeks. Their blood filled a crevasse deep enough to bathe in.

One fragment of verse by Polygoras survives: "The green fields lie ploughed like her thighs, the night is cold, O my love, I am coming." Those who do not see the war in such lines, Herodotus writes, have not known war.

Chorus

They rode cold gusts down in a blustered roaring

I'd withstood, all wind, with so much still to ask—

were they visitations or figments, intruders

or guests? Was it form they took in the swarm

or was form taken after? "We drift against,

O!, granite keels, and are so so cold," cried one

against the thunder. I flinched. Icy rain

gattling the leaves, raking a bruised light

over the lawn. But had they come to others

as to me? Did they lack all lineament

when they left? "Lo! what we went through

was not what we thought!" howled another;

and: "Leaving is not how we think it to be!"

Each hollered down a din of such mock,

muckery, gust. Had they nothing to say? "Observe

the birds' ferocious *fart*—" sniggered the first;

I threw up my hands and stormed away.

Dr Johnson's Table Talk

Truly, Sir, if ever I met an arse-picking pickle-fingered mettle-felcher—

———————

Indeed you are correct, Sir:
he was birthed in a shite-barn's shine-bowl.

———————

Not, Sir, upon my word: I should say not!

———————

That he is a shrivelled sock of skin, Sir, no man could doubt;
but so fast dribbled out—!

———————

Nay, Sir, not he; he would lose his arse if it were loose.

———————

Not hobbled, Sir; merely a three-legged dog piggered rearward.
Lacking a leg he hobbles the harder.

                                  Which leg! Which leg, she asks!

———————

I beg pardon, Sir? How is that?

———————

A gapstop, Sir! A gutter-slinger, Sir! A gross-bellied blowsy bin, Sir,
whose panny giggers wide for any with a pound!

———————

Sir: never did such a doddering gog-brained codfish come
so completely through a man's mud-shoaled pratts.

———————

His gaying instrument, Sir? I should say so!

———————

Ah, what is this? Roast duck? Pudding and pie?
Madam, a man would piss in his fist for a piece of this pie.

Plumb

What we went
through was not
what we thought.
That was then.
Then was not
what went on
but what stood
still. What stood?
Fall for one.
Fixed sway. Light.
Plunging straight
out of ourselves
what did not fade
fell true
in that slow
fall of our few
our unfathoming
days.

Odds Were

That swaggy haze of August heat
we limped through lugging bases, bats,
bitten leather mitts rubbed to a sheen
come dusk. Who we were. What we'd be.

High over shingled roofs vapour trails
drifted off into meaning. Faint screel
of the old dayliner, chinking downtrack.
It was taken back, all of it back.

A white white arbutus sun-stained
and shriven. What is and is again
is there, though it fades. Seen afar,
seems fire in its own dissolving fire.

We do not know if anything ends.
Soils leech, lakes rise, while in frail vials
men grow skin out of its own death.
But the loft of a ball on its right course,

a haft hefted in gripped fists, a bat
all riflecrack and gut-shivering hit
and the wood through no effort of its own
connecting. We just swung and ran.

Kid

...and morning bent our fender back, in,
chrome all warpled with unwashed light. Light
is what we come to, rundown in darkness.
Kid's hair in the glass streaming a greasy shine.
I turned the motor over: clouds of bright
birds burst the trees. What was ours, what parked us
there, what the hour: like any weekend cued
in that second reel of our lives, bored, beered,
unbuckled and bent double as in a pew,
shivering and all agrin. We shifted into gear,
the clack of hollow cans cruppled in the back
gone stale. How we moved through a savage light
blinded, amoan and bad-headed. Eyes fucked.
Fists swollen. God but that sun was bright.

The Boy Next Door

Because our ladder's battered leg banged, lurched,
listed badly, his head would slur a blurred
arc across the glass, dip, then disappear
to a bucket perched below. Maybe safety
mattered more to my mother than to me;
for pouring warm from bed I'd peer out, pale
fists pressed to the sill until his hands slid back
in view, vinegared, red-fleshed. He'd clank
up the ladder's steel slats, whorl soaped moons
into that glass, then scrape all crookedly off
with the long sinewy languor of a dream:
to my sleep-gogged eyes he seemed not to clean
the windows, but erase them. Always early
Saturdays, always at my waking,
the quiet rasp of wet cloth rubbing glass, then
the dull screel of dried rubber dragged across.
That boy next door a blur behind drenched hands—
and always the window again made whole.
As if I could step through. Stand there in his cold
uneasy air.
              But nights under no moon
low moans waded the witchgrass in our yard.
I'd stare at the glass through terrified air, watch
his slow drift through lamplit rooms,
the cautious countable lights going out behind
his blown head. Loose, wild, breathing murder
in my bed, feeling a fierce elation clockwork
through my skull. That was blood, rising.

Chorus

A clatter as the desk creaked, filling;

rattle of a handle at my knee. I felt

a presence passing: its rasping ceased

near the door. "Do not turn; do not turn

toward us," they coughed from awful throats,

crackling like nightbirds in the black.

What's happened? I grasped the lamp to lift it.

They had altered. "Do not turn that on,"

one hissed. And this: "He thinks *we've* turned."

I shivered. "What's t-turn t-t-turning

in him turns him p-pale," stuttered a second.

"You called us down and drew us here,"

the fiercest whispered, "*you* ordered *us*."

I'd ordered nothing. "And without order

is there art?" A low grimacing leer,

the air ashimmer at its edges. "He fears

the order's not his own." "Or not his

to own." "Or not his only." I feared only

what I'd failed to feel in my skin, let alone

in any other's. That I feared. "And?"

Already they were withdrawing. And.

And shouldn't I be more in it? I asked.

"You're in it regardless." I felt

something, a heat at my cheek, like a lantern

just cooling in the burn, from which

I understood they would, in the rhyme, return.

Late Rehearsal: Requiem in D Minor

Shade

that shapes stage,
wrist that takes shape: what dark
strings stretch gut-tuned to mark
page

by flecked page
each stagelight's seepage
to black? We are passage,
age,

sweet decline,
the sorrowful woods
shirr; we char when we should
shine.

Offstage fades
to wisp, white matchsticks
snapped in the strike; spark-flicked
frayed

seats catch, creak
where grey faces fold
close to scratch out each cold
sheet,

where horsehair
bows bend oarlike, slice
dripping a drenched silence.
Here.

Soft. A sound
of stunned pigeons aloft
in dark rafters: applause—
then

slow white hands,
faint, as if adrift
over black waters: Let lift,
it sings,

be light.

The Second Magi Returns to Parthia

Fallen ill my King and failing, I feared
we should not reach Judea: that strange flared
star seemed ever to falter, its cold light
near enshrouded night after icy night
in those bleached dunes. Lost, wind-rippled
in a grinding dark, our caravan ground on,
a weird eel unwinding windward in the lee;
and we rode what we hoped was west.

Any would founder. Frozen wadis, the bray
and crunch of camels lurching in the flail
and some nights the tracks six-toed, strange,
the cold tugging at our robes and how we
turned, always, to nobody there, just a creak
and shatter of iced reins
in half-flensed hands—

                      Like sand or rust
all corrodes; we last just long enough to outlast.
Forty nights, withering in darkness, it bore us
westward with it: we could not my King not
cross; each dusk the glittering sands spun
as we staggered out over eerie dunes,
rags on sticks under westering skies, red eyes
fixed on a plummeting sun.

Stations of the Geode

I

This world is hollow; go.
Break it. Under a barnacled dark
a hard light quartzes a queer fire:
  break it. Go. The true geode
grows against itself, is maculate,
scarred, all mar and grunt of stone,
  all glottal stop of rock.

II

Break it. Go. The true geode's
guts glint fluke-fanged, fixed-fast, agleam
in an amethyst crust of unrock,
  blooming like blown glass. Light
too can be entombed. Look: geodes
inlode with longing: what once was
  stone is stone still yet grows.

III

Blooming like blown glass, light
illumines the outer object alone.
Gripped in warm hands, glows warm
  what is utterly not us,
and beautiful: an egg furrowed,
infolded. How we long to go
  in where there is no in

IV

that is not utterly us,
our bodies but striate and shear.
Let us be air-scour, wind-wawl,
    an eye that won't open;
let us some nights let grief drill deep
in us, that it come back black,
    hollowed-out in wonder.

V

The eye that won't open
sees nothing. Here the heart's sump
thrumps its own slow erosions—
    vein-whorpled, ventricled,
blood-bellowing all with light.
We are bone-caged and vugulate,
    world. Break us
                to make us bright.

At the Edge of the Visible

In strange cities sometimes it happens. A statue parts the pigeon-stained curtain of its body and peers out in hard sunlight, amazed. In Stuttgart the living statues followed us with their eyes, bronzed arms upraised in benediction. I had been reading Boswell with a knuckle marking the page. How Dr Johnson had refuted Berkeley's argument against matter by kicking a stone over cobblestones. I refute it *thus*, he is supposed to have said. Sometimes the world's beauty overwhelms, and still we doubt our place in it. In the late October sunlight you rested a gloved hand on a saint's thigh and laughed. The statues could not help themselves, and looked away. Later, at the café in the park: an old man in a grey suit, folded over a chessboard, unmoving for hours. *Don't stare*, you whispered, and kicked my shoe. So that I was, in that place, for that hour, irrefutable.

Transparencies

Then slurred shut the sliding
door. Sunbleached

deck, weeds seething gold:
here what feeds

in the rooms of the world
wants no truck

with grace. Won't even
try. Too much light sears

the flesh; here
you lived eclipsed

by a cast back
glance. Your whole life

a rising from.

II

So morning stokes
its kiln. So you stake

this acre
of sky, this gulp

of flesh you gave
your days to. Nothing

is yours by right.
From white bells wasps

hove past pollened
with fury, all touch

and go. Wait. In the furnace
of itself it pitied

you: your peeled back
burned was the blessing

of its terrifying hand.

III

Handed a half-
glass you held out for the whole

of it all
day. In that cold water

a watery skin spun sky
in silvered fractals

of ice. Your skin spun
too. To sip, sip, stare, to

feel the day's fire anew: grace
is not the rivering of ice

down a cold glass in summer, is not dark
rings rising off a deck in heat,

is nothing. Who knew turning away
was ever your way. Doubt?

Doubt you knew.

IV

In the cantled deck's shade
your shade conceals

its meaning. You lean far
out. The pine railing suffers

in the flushed heat. Here
its brown paint finger-divots

soft in the grain where gripped.
Crows cluster out on the wires.

Utterly you imagined
this. Utterly you thought

stripping your life of you
might slip you more

fully in it. In the burning
yellow grass below

nothing stirs.

V

You lived for a time
unfrightened in sunlight, lived

white and searingly alone.
Planks of light hammered the deck

under your feet. You stood
in it. You stood in it

and burned
What good are our gifts

if the world is going
out regardless?

The world is going out,
the world is going out.

Pass, pass, you who lived burning, in it for a time.

Mediterranean Light

I

Then we stepped down out of the paintings, into our lives. It was already night on the terrace. The light from some stars is so old, our guide said, it set out before the human race had language. I was leaning over the stone balustrade and did not look up. In the paintings of Tintoretto there is a light that shines down onto the folds of fabric and a light that shines forth from it. That light, too, is much older than it appears. And somewhere it is still moving, you murmured. I was standing so close I could feel the heat coming off your skin. That was the heat of an afternoon sunlight now passed. Our guide looked at me and said: If the perspective is not right, you must change where you are standing. I watched you reach down and adjust the soft ankle strap of your heel and I could not think of where that elsewhere might be.

II

She stared at her feet,
     poured past him
wearing her winter

coat; he wanted to see
     her hips as she
came at him but couldn't.

III

In the station were so many voices, all talking at once. We gripped our bags close, fearing thieves; blinked through the iron grillwork at the great clock. A rush of warm air on our faces as each train punched past, not stopping, hurtling on into the earth. As if there were some more luminous world beyond this one. This world hurtles through space at speeds nearly unimaginable, yet our lives can remain motionless for years. When the doctor ran the cool sonogram over your belly we heard the hard fast footsteps of a second heart. That was the sound of our own new selves running towards us. On the platform a voice was shouting out destinations but we could not see where because of the crowd and because we were so much in it.

IV

Her wrists: a scent of split cedar in rain.
    A wash of winter traffic in the drapes;
shadows eating her face like emulsion.

—In the movies it's more romantic
to have glasses for reading
than for driving,
                    she said.

—Come into the light,
                    he said.

V

Later, alone, in southern Spain. Thick in the interval all day between your name and what I wanted to write. As the sun

was going down I stood from my desk and saw them, three
swifts, the soft oily knives of their wings slicing the sharp air
between the fig trees and twists of cacti. *This-this-this*, their
quick turnings urged. Articulate in their uncluttered syntax of
flight. The sun would be just rising in your life. In the gold light
of evening the night before you'd walked down by the lagoon
and seen the soft small yellow goslings following their mothers
through the weeds, as our daughter shifted inside you. In the
gold light of my own evening I put a hand to your belly and felt
her kick.

VI

Stunned, at the known edge of his life

at last, light took, flared
in fired ochre jars of clay
left cracked in the creaking
orchards at Mojácar.

Memory rakes its rocky
earth, sets everything
to echoing. In the leaves
the lit Spanish pears fill

like warm eyelids in the shade.

Omens at Dusk in the Year of the Dragon

Crying then, lifting like smoke off the grass.
A dark river through black air.
Black loons in fall, not many, but all

in the cold and the grey flooded fields
taken back. We stood taken back.
My white hand in yours cutting the bracken

and yellow larchgrass for home. The seeped
marsh-mud like a wound, closing. For the world
is not suffering only

and living is not how we think it to be.

Notes & Acknowledgements

The epigraph is taken from Robert Hass' poem "Winged and Acid Dark."

"Orpheus Ascending" appeared in *The Malahat Review*. "The Second Magi Returns to Parthia" appeared in the *Victoria Times Colonist*. My thanks to the editors for their support.

This book would not have been possible without the support of the Canada Council for the Arts and the BC Arts Council.

Thanks are due as well to Fundación Valparaiso, where several of these poems were worked, in part or in whole.

★★★

Thanks are due also to:

Kitty Lewis, Alayna Munce, Barry Dempster, and everyone at Brick Books for their enthusiasm and support; Michel Vrana for his gifted eye; my extraordinary editor, Sue Sinclair, for her care and grace; John Baker, Carla Funk, Jeff Mireau; Kevin, Brian, Josie, my parents Bob & Peggy, and always, overwhelmingly, Esi.

S teven Price's first collection of poetry, *Anatomy of Keys* (Brick Books, 2006), won the Gerald Lampert Award and was named a Globe & Mail Book of the Year. His first novel, *Into that Darkness* (Thomas Allen), was published in 2011. His work has been translated into several languages, including German, French, and Hungarian. He teaches writing at the University of Victoria.